Cont~

Preface - I wrote this book because of 2

Dedications...4

Chapter 1 - Branded..6

Chapter 2 - 'You only get a minute better live while you're in it. Cause it's gone in a blink'. "The Older I Get" by Alan Jackson 12

Chapter 3 - Dare I? 16

Chapter 4 – 'Jean Swain go conquer the world' he said. 'Jean, were you educated in this country?' she said..19

Chapter 5 - Our amazing son Stu 21

Chapter 6 - Keep on Moving 25

Chapter 7 - Glutton for punishment so what's next?.......................28

Chapter 8 - Birmingham here I come!...30

Photos 33

Chapter 9 - Our methods are different, but our hearts are the same.................43

Chapter 10 - More about this book. Origin of the book title 45

Chapter 11 - Questions and Answers with a difference......................47

Chapter 12 - A Message for Dyslexics..54

Specific Learning Difficulties (Dyslexia/Dyscalculia) Assessment Report 56

Author's Apologies 61

Preface - I wrote this book because of my Dad

Thanks, Dad, for showing me there were no witches in the garden. When I was little, and I thought there were witches in our garden, Dad taught me there were not. He told me instead they were wise women, often with a cat for company because they were lonely. Living in the woods because they understood the healing properties of plants. He taught me to confront things not to run away from them.

I thought I would like to make a speech at our son's wedding, unusual I know for the groom's mother. Our son is an incredibly unique and self-less character who got into trouble when he was younger. I felt that I wanted to share some of his stories to show that his intensions were honourable. I was lucky my son and his wife were both in agreement, although they may have been secretly dreading what I was going to say. I knew I would need some help.

I lived in London at the time and applied for a course at the Bishopsgate Institute to improve my public speaking skills. Sadly, I cannot remember the name of the course or the name of the tutor, but it was amazing. After the wedding, I received a letter from my cousin Janet S. I cannot remember the precise words, but she wrote something like initially she thought it might be a disaster (as did we all including me) but that it was actually a triumph.

Much later in lockdown when the Covid-19 pandemic hit the world, I had the time to look at the Bishopsgate Institute once again for inspiration. I found an online course entitled 'Power and Struggle stories of resistance in Britain' and applied. I was worried, because I have a hearing problem, so I mentioned it. They took it very seriously and adapted the presentation by adding subtitles which were very much appreciated. Although I mentioned my hearing problem, I had not mentioned my dyslexia. I suppose I got used to thinking I was just stupid and slow, compared to others. What I learnt at that first session was so powerful, as, when they covered disability, they included dyslexia. It made me reassess my whole life. I was absolutely amazed I must have had a very narrow definition of disability as when that word is mentioned my thoughts usually turn to physical disabilities. It made me realise, that dyslexia can be insidious and impact upon every area of your life. At that point, I wondered whether I could write a book. It does seem very self-indulgent and compared to what others are going through it might seem trivial. After careful thought, I decided to go ahead.

I wanted to write this book as a tribute to Eric, Stu and Dad, to thank all the other people in my life who have helped and encouraged me like Mum, Anne and Auntie Peggy and to confront my dyslexia as my dad taught me to.   Finally, I hope that out there somewhere, there might be just one dyslexic person who has felt inadequate all his /her life and has stumbled upon this book and like me found their 'lightbulb moment'.

Dedications - **In memory of Jason Helly**

So many people have helped and encouraged me throughout my life it is not possible to mention them all. But I am particularly indebted to the following:

Eric: You have always been my rock and had my back. Whatever foolhardy scheme I decided to embark on you encouraged and supported me. Thank you. MBLLOBA

Stuart: You are our world.

Fi: It was written in the stars that you would be our daughter in law.

Mum: You were wonderful no one could have had a better Mum than you.

Dad: Who taught me to confront my fears, who completely understood me and told me I would get there just in my own way, in my own time and to never, ever ever give up.

Sister dear: We were so lucky to have such brilliant parents and such a happy childhood.

Auntie Peggy: Who was always there for me echoing Dad.

Josie: If only you ruled the world, it would truly be a utopia.

Susie and Rodney: Thank you for coming with me and Eric to the funeral Parlour to say a last goodbye to Dad and having a toast to him afterwards. I really believe we can change the world with kindness.

Phil A: very special friend who was the first to recognise my dyslexia and help me.

Christine R: Thank you so much for a wonderful lifelong friendship which I treasure.

Moriom: The kindest person I know. "Imagine…. One day the world will be as one" by John Lennon

Julie: My amazing American friend. Thank you so much for making and sending me that special necklace and for the phone call you arranged during what was a very difficult time for me.

Maureen (my second mum), Joe and Uncle Wilf: Thank you for all the time and love you lavished on me during my childhood. I have never forgotten Joe that it was you who taught me how to fry an egg properly.

Carolyn and Pauline: My fantastic sisters. Thank you. I don't believe you have to have blood ties to be family.

Sue: We have had some fantastic holidays together such happy memories! Although deciding to trek to Zimbabwe without a guide was probably not one of our best decisions!!

Father Andrew: So hard working who embodies goodness with a gentle humour and acceptance for all.

To the lady on the bridge: I hope you find happiness.

Sandra and Jenefer: Without you this book would not have been written or published. Thank you from the bottom of my heart for your patience and encouragement.

Chapter 1 - Branded

'…in practice the secondary modern came to be seen as the school for failures. Those who had "failed" their eleven plus were there to learn rudimentary skills before advancing to factory or menial jobs.'

Wikipedia contributors (2021) *Secondary Modern School*. Available at:
https://en.wikipedia.org/wiki/Secondary_modern_school

I was born five years after the second world war ended. It was a time of austerity, rationing and appearances. I remember as a youngish child walking down the street and absent mindedly putting my hands in my pockets. A neighbour came up to me and told me in no uncertain terms that to put your hands in your pockets amounted to being a teddy girl and to removed them immediately.

She frightened me half to death. I probably did not even know what a teddy girl was, but it sounded very bad. I was terrified she would tell my mum and dad. I would not have liked them to think badly of me. I loved them both dearly as I did my little sister Anne. She was beautiful and is to this day. Blond hair and very petite.

 I lived in Thornton Heath in a large house in Manchester Road, with a lot of occupants, all relatives. It was so cold: no central heating in those days. My dad who was amazing at so many things, really struggled with house repairs. We had what we called a sky light in the roof. I found it comforting to look up and see the sky, but it had its downside. It leaked very badly indeed. No matter how hard my dad tried, and he did continue to try year after year (my dad was no quitter) he could not repair it. Paying for someone to come in and mend it was beyond our means, instead when it rained, we put an old tin bath underneath, surrounded by towels, and caught the downpour that way. I think this continued until the day they moved.

When I was about four, I stayed with my mum's sister for a short while. I am not sure why.   She was called Auntie Doris, married to Uncle Charlie and they had a daughter Janet three years older than me. While I was staying with them, we went on some sort of parade. Dressed up, myself as a fairy and Janet as a traveller. Someone took a picture of us. People looking at that photo now often remark I look cross, and I have to agree.

In reality, I was just a very quiet, self-conscious child who wore a perpetual frown, not because I was cross but because I was worried hence the nickname 'Worry Pot' in later life. I often could not understand what I should be doing, so did nothing rather than the wrong thing. This often mistakenly meant I was labelled lazy. Actually, I was anything but, to this day however I have real trouble with instructions (machines like the washing machine or the tumble dryer are my enemies).

I started school when I was 5. I only remember a few things. Once a boy being canned in front of the whole class, really terrifying. Taking the register back to the Headmistress' room and when she asked me my name not answering just standing there, my face getting redder and redder on the verge of tears. Cleaning the blackboard and being sick and being kept in at playtime for not doing enough work. Not the happiest of times.

Back then, there was a test called the 11 Plus Exam which all pupils sat in their last year at primary school. The results decided whether the pupil would go to a Secondary Modern School (for those that' failed' the exam), a Technical School (there were very few of these) or a Grammar School (for those considered to be academically able).

It must be amazing to be 'the first' to do something: to build a skyscraper or to climb Mount Everest. To be the first in your family to fail your 11 Plus does not have the same ring about it. In reality, I don't know whether I was the first to fail or just that it felt like that. Anyway, the shame of it! I cried for weeks and weeks. Friends tried to tell me that perhaps 'your letter' is still in the post as they sent you a letter if you 'passed'. Poor Uncle Wilf questioned me asking if I was top of the class why did I fail? I tried to explain I may have been top of the class, but I was in the B stream. It was mostly children in the A stream that passed their 11 plus.

My mum gently asked me what I had been asked to do during the exam. I said I did not really know, as mentioned previously to this day I find both written and spoken instructions hard to follow, so I wrote a story about being kidnapped by a sailor. I seem to remember there was a story about this doing the rounds at the time and it had captured my imagination so I thought the examiners might like my take on it. Sadly not. I was going to a Secondary Modern school.

I remember with sadness a friend who, a couple of years or so earlier, had also 'failed'. Her father was, I think, in politics. He did not speak to her for nearly two years. What a cruel system to label a child a failure at 11. Once I had got over the humiliation, I remember sitting at my school desk and thinking I am going to be a teacher and in my class, no one will be made to feel a failure. I did not tell anyone as I knew they would think the likelihood of me achieving that was nigh impossible. But I knew it was going to happen and years and years later it did.

One of the presents parents bought for their children if they passed the 11+ was a bike. I had wanted a bike for ages and 11+ failure or not, one Christmas I was lucky I got my wish. I was a selfish child and once I had discovered the bike I looked around for more presents. Alas only the bike! My mum and dad were extremely hard workers but not that well paid. It had probably cost them an absolute fortune. We took it outside and I was allowed to ride in the road. Dad told me, 'Ride to the end of the road, put your right hand out and turn right'. Easy-peasy I thought. In my world I had done just that only to find my dad running after me shouting something. In reality, I had put my right hand out but turned left. I was thought a danger on the road and my bike was taken away from me for ever. I was really thankful, although I had longed for a bike having to actually ride it entailed more than I thought. And I had only really wanted one because other children had one.

We lived close to a church and as soon as I was old enough, I became a Girl Guide. I enjoyed the Brownies their forerunner but really come into my own at Girl Guides. I had friends there, quite a few. I think by then I might have been a patrol leader no less. Once a month we had Girl Guide church parade. All the guides and their leaders attended the Sunday morning church service. At the beginning of the service the guides marched up the aisle one of us at the front carrying our flag. It was received and placed where everyone could see it. We took our seats for the service. Then when the service finished, we reversed the process. I had been asked to do a reading from the bible which filled me with anxiety, nevertheless it was an honour to be chosen. Success comes in various ways. I might be a failure at school but not at guides. I had forgotten the saying 'Pride comes before a fall'.

Earlier on, on that Sunday before going to church, I asked my mum if she could please 'test me' as I wanted to get it right without any mistakes. I chose the wrong time to ask a terribly busy lady. She worked in Woolworths only getting Wednesday afternoons and Sundays off. The former, she visited her Mum who lived in Morden on a council estate. My

Nana had a great friend there. They had been friends it seemed like for ever but nevertheless until the day Nana died, she only ever called her Mrs Capp and Mrs Capp only ever called Nana, Mrs Lambson. No first names were ever permitted, formalities reigned.

Most Sundays the lovely Auntie Peggy (who was so much fun), her husband Uncle Alf (a tall, well-built man), who said very little, but had a great sense of humour which, a young girl like me, could appreciate) and their daughter Linda, visited. Not just for dinner but also for tea. My mum always cooked a mouth-watering roast and we listened to the wireless while eating. I don't think I appreciated the programmes but everyone else seemed to. It was quite a ritual listening to Billy Cotton's Band show. Every show began with the same words: 'Wakey Wakey'! It was almost obligatory for us all to join in.

Tea was another matter. Often my dad made cheese on toast using his own cheese recipe. It was so tasty. Uncle Alf liked winkles. I was given the great honour and indeed I did feel immensely proud of getting the winkles out of their shell with a pin for him. Thanks to Uncle Wilf we had a television in the house. Not everyone had one back then and if memory serves me rightly (which sadly it often doesn't) it was in black and white. Uncle was not there on a Sunday, but we were still able to watch it. It was a far cry from today's television which offers so many different channels as well as being able to record things to watch later. As I recall, we only had two channels, but I am open to correction.

Back to Mum and her busy life. She had a huge house to clean and an open fire in the grate to clean out each night, ready to be lit the following day. She cooked all our meals from scratch, so potatoes to peel and boil, vegetable to be prepared and cooked. With stuffed hearts, sausages or liver and bacon. Most days she rushed home from work and didn't even have time to remove her coat before she began cooking. No wonder I was getting so fat. In addition to the main course, she made the most marvellous suet puddings. Which took an age to cook I remember she boiled them and had to keep refilling the saucepan with water. But it was worth it. She would take the white china basin out, turn it upside down and pat it and somehow it would turn out whole. Then she would pour syrup over it and using a very sharp knife, would divide it into portions. Finally, after all the waiting with our mouths watering, we would all dive in.

But I digress, back to Girl Guides where I was so happy. That Sunday morning, mum just did not have the time to listen to me but made encouraging noises saying I would be fine. I do not remember much. Only, that at the allotted time getting out of my seat, walking to the front, and reading the piece I was asked to read. All in all, I thought it had gone quite well. The service carried on until it was the Vicar's turn, he started his sermon. I was not really listening properly. I was a dreamer, even then. But suddenly, what he said, caught my attention. I felt myself redden (not for the first time, not the last time either). He was talking about my reading! I saw people look at me and it was not the admiring looks I had hoped for in fact, the person next to me was nudging me and a few other guides were laughing. That was until Captain put her finger to her lips and in no uncertain terms made a loud shushing sound.

What did the Vicar say? I was unable to digest it at first. I had been practicing the reading ever since I was asked, and mum said I would be alright. Apparently, I had called somebody by the name of Simon when he was actually called Simeon. I suppose I had put the poor Vicar in an impossible position. He had no option but to correct me in front of everyone. I wanted to run from the church and would have done, but I was sitting in the middle of a row, and it would be so difficult to have to shuffle past everyone. Instead, I did the usual thing I went redder, and redder, hung my head in shame and refused to look at anyone. Then, once the service was over, I made a bolt for home. Where, as I did not want to incur further humiliation, I pretended my reading had been perfect.

However, life went on and Susan, my friend from Guides, still liked me miraculously. I did not really like to mix with grammar schoolgirls I suppose I felt inadequate, but I liked Susan I thought she was different, so it was alright. She introduced me to many things, and in return I introduced her to Norman Wisdom. One of his films was being shown at the local cinema. I forget which one. We decided to go together on Saturday afternoon. It was a great treat and something to look forward to.

We duly met up, paid for our tickets, then feeling very grown up we sat in our seats and eagerly awaited the film. In those days they had an A film and a B film. You really got value for money! The film began and Susan did what most other people were doing: laughed and laughed. I tried to do the same. Only suddenly, I did not get the joke anymore, I didn't think it was funny at all. It seemed quite sad instead, a little man getting laughed at all the time. I started to feel sorry for him possible not the film maker's intention at all.

Chapter 2 - *'You only get a minute better live while you're in it. Cause it's gone in a blink'*. "The Older I Get" by Alan Jackson

Almost every minute of every day (or so it seemed to me) that I was in secondary school this dreadful fear hung over me. It sounds implausible, melodramatic even, but it was true. How could I possibly tell her my secret, she would not understand. So, I carried on looking at her but remained silent. 'Jean, I am going to ask you one more time and this time I want an answer! Why are you always late for school you don't live that far away?' She went on to explain that she was always on time, and she lived a lot further away than I did.

I really liked this teacher and I think she was genuinely concerned and perplexed. I wish I could have explained, but I just couldn't. Yes, to my recollection everyone else in the household left much earlier than me and I was responsible for getting myself to school. Yes, I was disorganised and a dreamer, nearly always running late for everything and I didn't like walking over the railway bridge, it seemed a bit lonely and dangerous. But there was an additional reason, I was literally terrified of going to school and 'them' finding out that I was not good enough for the C stream, the lowest stream and being sent to a special school. I thought that as long as nobody knew except me, how stupid I was, I could avoid what seemed to me that terrible fate.

Also similar to Primary school, I was perplexed by their teaching methods, that I was convinced were not for the best for everyone. In fact, it made a lot of people give up the ghost and I was one of them. Every single week we had a maths' exam and every time, the results were read out loud in class. The same pupils were top, and the same pupils were bottom. In the end, I would give the paper a cursory glance, realise I couldn't do it and spend the time looking out of the window. It was not ever a nice view just the top of the school canteen. There was no effort to help those like me who were struggling, to improve. There was no effort put into stretching the ones that 'performed well'. So those that struggled, gave up and those that were at the top become complacent.

In my final year at school aged 15 with no qualifications I was interviewed by somebody not quite sure who it was, who asked me what I wanted to do, and I said I'd like to be a gardener. A week or so later dressed in a yellow twin suit and a tweed skirt, I was being interviewed for an office job that I knew I was totally unsuited for. They decided to employ me and I'm sure must have regretted it. I struggled with the filing and everything else I really disliked it! Jobs were easy to find in the mid-60s so I left and found a similar office job, I wasn't much good at that either!

However, it was when I was working at one of these office jobs that I met Eric on a blind date we went to Brighton. I was 16 he was a bit older. I have still got the present he bought me for my 17th birthday. My mum loved him right from the start if we ever argued and we are so different we did and still do argue, she always took his side. My dad and Uncle Wilf were not quite so keen. I encouraged Eric to grow his hair really long. It was all the fashion in those days.

Every time he came to pick me up Uncle Wilf who lived with us would shout down from the top of the stairs 'Get your bloody haircut'. He was also known to yell at the top of his voice 'Shut that bloody door were you born in a barn?' And 'Turn those bloody lights off' if we ever dared to leave a room and forgot to turn them off. He was a character and I loved him dearly. He never frightened me he was just trying to teach us to be thrifty and not waste money.

We got married in 1970. I remember just before midnight the day before our wedding Auntie Peggy and I walking down to Beulah Road. Even between the two of us we struggled with the heavy bags of dirty laundry. We finally got to the launderette, which was empty, put the washing, then the coins in. The machines started. I used to find the tumble dryers mesmerising watching them going round and round. I can only guess that poor mum had so much to do (probably lots of relatives were staying) that the 'laundry duty' was assigned to me and Auntie Peggy!

Neither Eric not I remember much about the actual day. What stays in my mind was leaving the wedding and popping back home to Manchester Road to change before going off on a honeymoon. (The honeymoon was unexpected someone had given us £50, and we borrowed Eric's firm's van and had decided to head to Cornwall).

We got there only to find neither of us had a front door key. But luckily there was a tall wooden side door that led to the back garden. I think Eric must have scaled that, then opened it for me to go in. We could not get in through the back door of the house though. The only way was through the kitchen window. It was the old-fashioned sash cord type luckily it was not locked. I remember in my wedding dress, complete with a very long veil I clambered through the window onto the kitchen table. The next day I told mum what had happened. She said she knew we had not got a key but that 'You are Eric's problem now'. She was confident he would sort it.

We spent the night at a small hotel, don't ask me how I did it but the next day I got up, dressed and whilst walking to breakfast fell down the stairs. Luckily, I did not hurt myself. We went back to Mum and Dads for Sunday dinner then left for Cornwall. Two things stand out. On the journey down we stopped to give a solitary young lady a lift. Then just like in a comedy film, five of her friends appeared out of the bushes. We somehow managed to get them all in and had a pleasant chat before dropping them off at their destination. We did encounter one other problem. I am not sure whether we had prebooked or was just taking a chance and hoping that we would find a B and B. But when we spoke to the owner of one and asked for a bed for the night, she said I looked too young to be married and she would not entertain having an unmarried couple in her B and B! So, we had to look elsewhere. I think at one stage the money ran out and we slept in the van.

But I digress again, back to my early working life. I think it was at this time my dad saw how unsuited I was for office work and how unhappy I was. I remember him telling me you have to be happy at work because so much of your time is spent there. He thought about it and said: 'Well, you like talking why don't you be a GPO telephonist?' So, I applied got accepted, completed the training, and started work at our local telephone exchange.

It did not happen very often but occasionally I was timetabled to take 999 calls. Funnily enough I don't remember being frightened. When I look back it seems so primitive. There was a light bulb above where we were sitting; it was painted blue. When anybody dialled 999 it flashed on and off. I remember we used to have to say: 'Emergency which service do you require?' before putting them through.

Chapter 3 - Dare I?

At that time if you worked for the government which I did as a General Post Office telephonist and were under 18 you were given day release to attend college. To either further your qualifications or as in my case to try to gain qualifications. I took English Literature and Language and failed both.

It intensified the feeling of failure I always felt. But looking back it was a big ask. I started the course halfway through. I had missed so much. I didn't even have a copy of the book we were studying until the tutor was kind enough to give me hers.

Also, as nothing was explained to me, I did not really understand why I was there or want to be there. I was out of my comfort zone. I didn't appreciate at that time the opportunity it was. But as ever it planted a seed.

Back to my 'work record'. I got restless so after a while I applied to work at the International Exchange in London. I remember I took phone calls from two famous people one was Yoko Ono and one Marvin Gaye both very polite and friendly. Another office job followed then when I was in my seventh job in eight years as a hospital telephonist, I became pregnant, had our son and as was customary in those days I stayed at home to look after him.

Stu was about 3 years old, possibly in kindergarten when I made a familiar journey. I took the 159 bus, got off and walked to the same college where I had previously failed my exams. As I walked past the Town Hall I glanced up and noticed the ANC (African National Congress) flag flying above the Town Hall. We had made a donation through a friend, although it was a banned organisation at the time it was to become 'unbanned' in 1990.

Eric and I had been on several anti-apartheid marches usually ending in Trafalgar Square where South Africa House is located. We were lucky enough to hear Archbishop Trevor Huddleston speak, a well-known anti-apartheid activist.

Friend Sue, Eric and I also went to the Fairfield Halls in Croydon to hear Archbishop Desmond Tutu speak, a remarkable man who I admire greatly. One of his messages was about not judging people and forgiveness. He said no one ever knows what another person is going through.

Meeting famous people whilst visiting the loo, when out and about, had happened before. So, it came as no surprise as when Sue and I nipped to the toilet during the interval that we met Wendy Craig a famous actress. She very nice, very friendly. We talked about a series on television that she had starred in called 'Butterflies'. Sue and I were both fans.

I had finally arrived at the college entrance, took a deep breath and ventured in, I was facing my nemesis, applying to retake the exams I had previously failed. I was taken to see a Mr Jackman who I had never encountered before. After the introductions, he explained that I would have to write a short piece of writing to make sure I was eligible for the courses.

I dithered. I had not anticipated this. Mr Jackman saw me hesitating he said something like if you don't at least try you'll always regret it. He was right so I picked up the pencil and wrote something very boring about myself. My name, age, hobbies etc then put the pencil down, handed him my written work and waited.

He told me it was okay, and it was not long after that I started GCE Literature and Language. The tutor seemed very young, I wondered what on earth he could teach me. (I had forgotten Desmond Tutu's message about not making judgements) I was soon to find out!

I found the course fascinating. One of his methods was to teach us through current events, it made the course more meaningful. We learnt about the Irish situation and The Women's Liberation Movement, things we could relate to. It was relevant and real.

We were even allowed if needs must, to bring our children. At one point I couldn't find anyone to look after Stu so he came in with me and was as good as gold. I wish I could remember the lecturer's name. He was remarkable, because of him I and the others did quite well. I got an A for English Language and a D for English Literature. The latter really annoyed me so a few months later I sat a re-take, and this time managed an A.

At the end of the course a report was written and given to us; there was a comment encouraging me to enrol for an A level. I had started the A-level course when another more appealing opportunity arose.

Chapter 4 – 'Jean Swain go conquer the world' he said. 'Jean, were you educated in this country?' she said

I looked at the piece of paper I picked it up and read it then put it down. I went away did something else, refused to think about it but sometime later was drawn back to it. Once again, I sat down at my desk, picked it up, it was small, rectangular with a caption and information written underneath. I re-read it for what seemed like the 100th time and wondered if I dared act on it, an application to apply for a Bachelor of Education course. There was something like an 'Exceptional Entry Procedure' where you did not need formal qualifications to apply. But you had to pass exams. It was now or never. I honestly cannot remember if I phoned or wrote to them the only two options to get in contact as far as I could remember back then.

It was not long before I found myself sitting at a desk taking an entrance exam. I waited nervously for the results. Miraculously, I had passed the English exam and also an IQ test, but bad news followed. I had failed the maths exam, but I would be allowed to retake it at a later date.

I found a little job cleaning in a small B and B on Sunday evenings. I did not mind cleaning, making beds and hoovering the rooms, but found it hard lugging the hoover up all the stairs (sadly there was no lift). And sorting the fridge contents, which was a task occasionally allocated to me, was also ok. But I hated with a vengeance having to empty and clean the ashtrays. Everyone seemed to smoke back then! But I was accruing money, which I spent on math's lessons. That enabled me to retake the maths exam and this time I passed.

I ended the course as I had started it: I passed in one area (teaching practice) but failed another (my final exam). History was repeating itself. But I had a second chance: I resat the exam. My tutor phoned me up shortly afterwards. He began by explaining that he had, had to 'fight my corner' but it was then I heard those magic words. 'Jean Swain go conquer the world' I had attended college and gained a Bachelor of Education degree. I would hardly ever bother to put that after my name, but now I was entitled to.

Not content with that, it had dawned on me that the problems I always had with English were not my only problems. I had difficulty with maths too. I remember once as ridiculous as it sounds, I mistakenly dialled my own number whilst thinking I was dialling a friend. The realisation came to me one day that I did that, because I do not see numbers, only patterns. So, if my phone number is written or said in the 'conventional way' I just do not recognise it, but I do recognise it if it is written in a special way,'my way'.

I thought I must be the only one to have this 'oddity'. But years later, we had someone working in our house, he overheard me explaining this to someone. He told me he was exactly the same. I decided at that point (glutton for punishment) to take my GCSE Maths at a daytime class close to where I lived. My dad's policy of facing up to things, was paying dividends.

It was during one of those lessons that the tutor turned to me and asked: 'Were you educated in this country, Jean?' I never knew why she asked or enquired but reassured her I was. I have struggled badly with maths all my life. Luckily, there were two people that 'rescued me'. Eric, who not only always had my back, but was really good at maths. He patiently explained things to me in a way that I could understand. But also, a friend, who happened not only to have a Bachelor of Education degree but also a Postgraduate Diploma in Special and Inclusive Education. She had recognised dyslexia and dyscalculia in me. She assessed me and wrote a report, which meant that I was given extra time in the maths' exam, as a lot of reading was involved. I was dubious about getting extra time, I thought it might be cheating, but was assured it was 'my right'. I passed. Another hurdle jumped successfully. The report is copied in full at the back of this book.

Chapter 5 - Our amazing son Stu

Just please let me do it my way I tried to do it your way it just won't work for me I showed our son who must've been about five at the time a picture of three elephants standing in a group, two small one large. His teacher had asked her pupils to identify the odd one out. The 'correct' answer was the large elephant. That was to everyone except our son.

I came home from Parents' Evening sat down with him and asked him why he had chosen one of the small elephants as the odd one out. Sometimes in life we see the obvious but don't delve deeper to find a solution. He had looked carefully at the picture facing the right stood one of the small elephants, facing the left stood the large and second small elephant. His answer was the small elephant on the right because he had looked at the direction the elephants were facing. And who was to say that was wrong!

We spent about eight? years in our first house until we moved not that far away to a bigger house. Stu was about 5 he had completed just over one year at Infant school. Although not that far away it was a different catchment area hence a different school. It had its advantages it was very close to home. He seemed to make friends easily and progressed through school. But we got more and more concerned about his reading. I am not sure why, but the teachers felt his progress was adequate. And I suppose there was some evidence that at that age boys were slower than girls at reading etc.

We continued to worry he was articulate and very intelligent why was his writing illegible, his spelling very erratic and why was he still struggling with reading? We went to the doctors they were sympathetic but not really able to help.

Finally, one Sunday my sister and her husband drove up to our house. It was kind of them they lived quite a long way from us and led very busy lives both teachers. We had arranged for Stu to have a private dyslexic assessment. I had spoken to a friend Teresa as we were both worried about our boys' lack of literary progress. She mooted the idea they might be dyslexic. It seemed to fit, hence arranging the assessment. It is very odd I had never thought before that Stu might be dyslexic in spite of my diagnosis. I never seem able to 'make links' like other people.

The report stated he had a high IQ and was indeed dyslexic. Once we had the diagnosis the arrangement was made for him to have (weekly I think it was) lessons with a qualified dyslexic teacher. Previously his class teacher had been giving him extra lessons. She was extremely kind and a very good teacher but not dyslexic trained.

He started at secondary school and seemed to enjoy it he was assessed by the local authority's education psychologist who confirmed his dyslexia and wrote a report. One of the things he recommended was working on a computer programme. Sadly, that did not seem to happen. I may be wrong, but I think when I spoke to the school, they mooted the idea of putting him in a remedial stream. I was horrified his IQ was high he did not need remedial teaching he needed specialist dyslexic teaching. If he had been remedial, we would have gladly agreed to the remedial stream.

Not that long after an open meeting took place with staff and parents from the school he attended. I asked what help he was getting and why his recommended computer sessions were not taking place? They replied there was a shortage of computers and a lot of boys needed help. It must be said there was one teacher who tried very hard to help him, but he had not had any dyslexic training. Stu was still struggling. We were in despair although he was personable, kind and intelligent if his literacy skills were lacking how would he get a job? It's the hardest thing we have ever done for all of us, we found a second property in Kent and a private school with a dyslexic unit attached. After taking an entrance exam he started school there.

We know we were extremely lucky to be able to do this so many people would not have been able to. Also, it went against our principles but having tried and failed to get appropriate help within the State system we felt we had no choice. It was very difficult for all three of us in very different ways. Eric, after driving all day drove down to be with us. He would arrive late in the evening. Have something to eat, watch a little bit of tv then sleep. He got up in the early hours of the morning to drive back to Croydon where he started his day's work. By Thursday he was so tired he stayed there but came down Friday evening to spend the weekend with us.

It was equally hard on Stu he was taken away from all his friends and the area he had grown up in and was familiar with. I wasn't much happier had qualified as a teacher, had never taught and wanted to teach in London. But it was worth its weight in gold. After completing the first year he said to us he was a bit of an outsider and that he wanted to board. We were unsure of his motive whether what he said was true or he saw the toll it was taking on all of us and this was his solution. Fast forward and Stu has a good job and is happily married. The best way to explain our son and his personality is to share a very shortened and very slightly altered version of the speech I made at his wedding.

Good afternoon, everyone. For those of you who do not know I am Stu's long-suffering mum. I think it's very brave of Stu to let me make a speech he has no idea what I'm going to say but this is payback time, be afraid Stu be very afraid. I would like to just give you a small flavour of what it has been like to be his parents, over the years the telephone has played a big part.

Ring ring ring ring 'Hi mum dad how are you?' 'We are fine how are you Stu?' 'Here's the thing' (we came to dread that phrase). 'I am in hospital I was cleaning out the milkshake machine (this was when he worked for a large burger chain) and I accidentally electrocuted myself'. And he had only popped into work to help out a friend!!

Ring ring ring ring. 'Hi mum, dad how are you?' 'We are fine how are you Stu?' 'Here's the thing'. Our hearts almost stopped beating. 'I am in a police station and have been arrested for robbery'. 'Did you do it'? 'Of course, I didn't'? Apparently, he had been working in a school and was in the playground when he saw a smoking safe. Knowing the pupils would be coming out from school soon, he run into the school kitchen and found a tea towel. He placed it over the safe and dragged it into the school. Told the Head Teacher who telephoned the police and waited for them to arrive. Unfortunately, when they did arrive the first thing, they did was to arrest Stu and take him down to the police station. It was sometime later that they realised they had made a mistake. Someone had seen him drag the safe inside the school and given his description to the police. Hence the arrest. No wonder we both went grey at a very early age.

Ring ring ring ring 'You answer it Eric?' 'No, you answer it Jean'. 'Hi Mum Dad, how are you?' 'Stu are you in hospital or a police station?' 'No' sigh of relief from both of us. 'Where are you? 'I'm at Oxford university, I'm a student here'. Long pause! 'Stu you and I both know you are not a student at Oxford university'. Silence! 'What are you studying then?' 'I can't study I have to hide in a room all day, but it was really good we had tea at the master's table last night, got to go bye'. The story was a friend got a place at Oxford university and was finding it difficult to fit in so Stu thought he would stay there a while to help the settling in process.

In my speech I made more references to his 'good deeds' and the new strategy Eric and I had adopted when the phone rang. Which was to run down to the end of the garden and pretend not to hear it. I then continued. 'And that was the light bulb moment when I realised that Stu was not like most of us, he does not walk by on the other side he is that rare person the good Samaritan. Who always stops and tries to help and that is why he was always getting into so much trouble. I continued by saying how much Eric and I loved him and to thank him for being such a wonderful generous and caring son over the years. Cautioned him about becoming too big headed and after welcoming Fi our daughter-in-law into the family finished by saying I hoped that they would be as happy as Eric and I had been over the years.

Chapter 6 - Keep on Moving

We said our farewells to our son after he had made the decision to board and reluctantly Eric and I returned home. In spite of all our reservations at leaving him my heart soared. I knew I would enjoy being back in London I'm a London girl always was always will be. But we missed our son terribly and the guilt was awful. What had we done abandoning our son in a private school in Kent, what sort of parents were we? However, he seemed to thrive he was made rugby captain of the school team and his house team. He seemed to really enjoy sports. I was really terrified though; rugby seemed such a physical game the potential for so many injuries. Again, the agonising had we made the right choice if he had stayed at the state school, perhaps he would never have played rugby and would be safer.

One bonfire night I remember looking out the window thinking what is Stu doing, where is he? If he had been here, we would have a bonfire in the garden with loads of fireworks and have friends and family round. It was only recently when I was going through boxes of things that I had not had time to unpack when we moved, that I came across a letter. I don't know why I had it or read it. I shouldn't of it was a letter from Stu to his grandparents (my mum and dad) belated apologies Stu! He seemed to be writing that he was having a lovely time and thanking them for sending him money. They must have written to him when he was away at school, I had no idea. He had penned a lovely reply. He went on to say it was very kind of them, but they should really send their money to Sarah (who was my sister's first child) rather than him. He reiterated not to worry he was having a good time (I seem to remember he made friends with somebody in the kitchen and was often offered seconds) and was happy. Thank goodness! One thing less to fret over as we get older and look back over our lives and see all the mistakes we made and regret.

Eric continued working as a salesman. Even though it was very long and demanding he was working Monday to Friday then every Sunday he would do his paperwork. Every Saturday without fail he would drive down and watch Stu play sports. Stuart never forgot that.

Once again, I'm not entirely sure about the timeline, which of these two schools I worked at first, but I think it was a local secondary school where I taught English part time once a week.   Then after a while I decided to change jobs (at that time there were so many vacancies for teachers) and taught at a primary, church school in Brixton. It was a part time English as an additional language teaching post. When I did my degree EAL had been one of my electives, so I did have some knowledge /training in that area. Again, I enjoyed it immensely but then I wanted another challenge. I think when you feel inadequate you are always trying to prove to yourself and others, your worth. Very little was/is really planned in my life I just seem to stumble across things and then jump in. I have always been terribly lucky and so far, things have nearly always worked out as it did in my next teaching job. I think it was in The Times Educational Supplement that I saw an advert for a full-time class teacher at a school in the East End. I applied and went to look around the school I was enchanted. The pupils were amazingly well behaved, all except three pupils hailed from Bangladesh and had English as their second language. The pupils called all the teachers by their first name. However, as some people who were against this (and it was actually the only school I've ever taught in where this happened) predicted this did not result in a lessening of respect.

I remember going to one teacher's class (she has since become one of my closest friends) and the children had made this amazing car out of cardboard. Whenever they wanted time out, they could just pop into the car. I don't think personally the pupils suffered from the lack of a National Curriculum.

I knew if we had any problems there were numerous members of staff, I could go to including the headteacher and deputy for guidance. One time I wasn't sure about the classroom layout, so I asked the Head to look at it for me he made one or two suggestions for improvements that I took up. And those days we did home visits after school where we got to know the parents and hopefully build up relationships. I made so so many mistakes but the technique they used to correct me was not only effective but very kind. I remember asking one pupil 'What is your Christian name?' I look back and squirm how could I ask a Muslim what their Christian name was? How stupid how thoughtless so ignorant! A teacher was standing nearby she corrected me by asking the pupil what her FIRST name was. It was only then the penny dropped. It was at this school I finally did my probationary year and passed. I became a fully-fledged teacher. Though I loved it there the time had come to move on to pastures new.

Chapter 7 - Glutton for punishment so what's next?

Stu received his GCSE results he could've stayed on, but we wanted him home and we like to think that he wanted to come home too. He moved back in learnt to drive got a car went to the local college and gained more qualifications. At this point Eric changed jobs and his interest in 490th bomb group (American airmen who were stationed here during the Second World War) intensified. He eventually became their Historian.

I saw an advert asking for English as an additional language teacher to apply and it was in the Croydon area, so I applied. For once not too much travelling! Although at that point I didn't have any EAL qualifications I did have experience of working with EAL pupils. I applied and was offered the job on a temporary basis initially but later that turned into a permanent contract.

I joined a huge organisation called The Multicultural Service which consisted of several teams one of them the EAL Primary team which I joined. We were so lucky. Not only was it very rewarding but there were opportunities to get qualifications and it was here I gained a 'Certificate in Teaching English Across the Curriculum in Multilingual Schools'. I also made a lot of lovely likeminded friends some of which I am still in touch with today.

We were each assigned several schools our tasks varied according to the needs of the pupils. We were able to spend time with them to identify their needs. Supply resources sometimes dual language occasionally go on home visits. Or accompany them on trips outside of school. We would sometimes go to the teacher's planning sessions and make resources helping to make the lessons inclusive.

Most things I decide to do take the same route. I look at something I think about it and reject it I'll pick it up again, think about it again, scratch my head a few times and then inevitably I'll jump in! Around this time, I was writing to a gentleman on death row. I was and still am a member of Amnesty International and it was in one of their magazines I saw that they were asking for people to write to death row prisoners, and I responded.

Our correspondence started his name was Bobby. In his first letter he wanted to know why I decided to write. The reason was I had read about the awful conditions in some US prisons and the racial injustices that occurred in their legal system We did write to each other for a while it was quite sporadic. My letters to him took ages and ages to write. Even when I thought I had finished I would re-read them for what I thought had to be the last time. Only to find I had duplicated some words and omitted others and sometimes it did not even make sense. My dyslexia means that everything I do takes so much longer than non-dyslexics although I did not know that at the time, and the results weren't even that good. My handwriting was awful so initially I think I used an old-fashioned typewriter. Then I changed to a computer. Spellcheck really came in handy! Much easier than having to use correction fluid!

I learnt a lot from his letters I am not sure how much if anything he got from my letters to him. Then one day he wrote to me and said he was going to waive his appeals. He wanted me to stop writing. I am not sure how I felt, I was worried for him and hoped I had not let him down, but I knew that some prisoners decide they cannot live with the constant uncertainty and the conditions that they live in. I think I felt that the right thing to do was to accept his decision. Looking back, I wonder whether I should have tried to get him to change his mind but ultimately it was his life and the decision had to be his.

I decided nevertheless to attend the forth coming Amnesty International meeting where we were told more about death row prisoners. It was at one of these meetings that I saw the leaflet. It was advertising a course. A Post Graduate Diploma in Immigration Law and Policy. It sounded really interesting I was working four days, but I could easily fit in an evening course. I had spoken to Eric and made up my mind to do it. The only slight problem being where it was being held, Birmingham.

Chapter 8 - Birmingham here I come!

Somehow it had all been arranged. I had enrolled on the course in spite of the far away destination and the lecturer in charge telling me people had applied from London before but none of them had ever finished the course. Little did she know that, that information just made me more determined to be the one that would!   At that time mobile phones were in their infancy. I looked at it, it was blue my favourite colour and enormous. Eric had bought it for me so that we could keep in touch.

The course finished fairly late at night fine if you lived local. But for me it would have been nigh impossible to get back home. So, I stayed overnight at a B & B recommended by the college.   The walk back from the college to the B & B was okay during the summer months when it was light. Quite another proposition though when it was dark, quite eerie! No pedestrians but a lot of noisy traffic whizzing by.

The course was amazing so well thought out and the lecturers excellent and approachable. A mixture of academia and practicality. Essays, presentations, debates the latter two making it very assessable to me. I learnt so much including one thing that horrified me and will to this day. The lecturer quoted a rhyme that was sung by children in the 1950s whilst skipping. It was awful I will not repeat it here it was/is racist and ends with the line '...go back. I racked my brains wondering whether I'd actually sung it or was just familiar with it. I certainly at that time had absolutely no idea what it meant. To my knowledge when we were in the playground or playing outdoors on the green at the top of our road no adult or anybody else approached us and told us what it was about and how wrong it was.

The other students were very friendly. Even so some of the time I was terrified. The other students all seemed so able and at that time essays were handwritten. My handwriting was and still is appalling. The words from my head come out faster than I can write them. Thank goodness for progress now I can dictate things into my iPhone. We were allowed up to 6 years to complete the course most completed it in 3. I took longer but can't remember how long. During that time, I had a hysterectomy and took a long time to recover. Also sadly coming home on the train from Birmingham one day there was quite a horrible incident. A group of lads rampaged through our carriage shouting, swearing, pushing one another, and insulting the passengers I found it really scary. I did not complete my journey I got off at an earlier station and went home. Once home I realised that I might be able to recognise them.

With hesitation a day or two later I went to the police station that was local to where I had got off the train. They were very pleasant but told me to contact the Transport police, I should have pursued it, but I didn't. It was wrong of me. I did however get in touch with Victim Support they sent somebody round. He was a nice guy we chatted things through one meeting was enough sometimes you just have to get back on the horse!

I don't know why I didn't go to the graduation ceremony, but I had decided not to. They sent the certificate through the post, which sad to say I promptly lost or rather it's somewhere in one of the many boxes I have left unpacked in the garage from when we moved almost 3 years ago!

I had really enjoyed being part of the Multicultural Service but decided to move on. I was approached by someone who was setting up a Refugee Advisory Team in Croydon and accepted the new job. She was an amazing manager, the best! Organised, fair, approachable and to this day a very good friend. The workload was really diverse. We went into both secondary (which I was not used to) and primary schools and I remember going into one Special school. The aim was to support the pupils/students in any and every way we could. We assessed them and wrote reports with recommendations. We tried to provide resources as often as possible dual language and to do home visits. We were in a privileged position. We often had the luxury of 1:1 teaching and time which sometimes allowed us to develop a relationship where students/pupils felt comfortable and able to confide in us. One of the things that I was told by a student was so awful that even today haunts me if I allow myself to think about it.

I was so lucky to be working with such professional, supportive, and patient colleagues. I was always asking their advice and counsel. In 2008 we were nominated and received an award from Croydon Council for 'Making a difference to the community'. See the next chapter for a taste of what it was like to work as a Refugee Advisory Teacher.

Photos

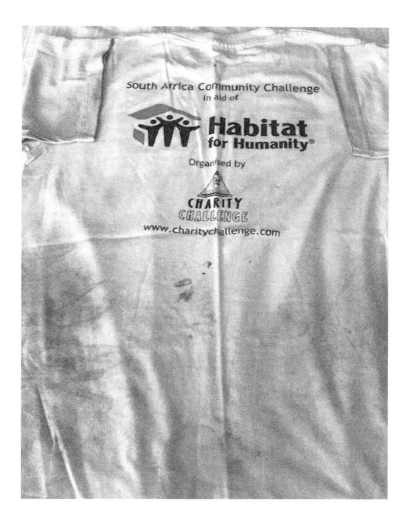

The t-shirt I wore when house building in South Africa in 2009.
I kept it and never washed it because it has the soil of South Arica on it.

Woman at work

Walking in a parade with my cousin Janet. Wearing that look on my face where people mistaken say I look cross. They are right I do look cross. However, in reality I am just bewildered and worried about doing the wrong thing.

An embroidered postcard sent from France during the First World War from my grandad to my nana

Model girl

A 25 year old brunette, Mrs Jean Swain of Norman Road, Thornton Heath, won the weekly Model Girl competition at Pontin's St Mary's Bay Holiday Village. She now qualifies for the all season finals later this year.

Carrying Stuart in my arms and not wearing my glasses so I couldn't see a thing. I entered a beauty contest and to everybody's surprise won.

My indomitable Nana and Grandad

My parents who I love so much

Our amazing son Stu

Dad was worried about us travelling abroad he had only been abroad once to France in WW2. In the morning just before our departure to Majorca he came round and gave me this St Christopher which I still have and cherish.

Born a rebel

Chapter 9 - Our methods are different, but our hearts are the same

Communication was at first difficult as we had no common language. My fault, I probably had forgotten to request an interpreter to accompany me. I don't think we were allowed to go on home visits solo. I sometimes puzzled over why my memory was so bad. And unlike some of the other Refugee Advisory / EAL teachers who had acquired at least a smattering of several languages I seemed unable to. I can honestly say of all the home visits I did as a Refugee Advisory teacher I only saw two that I thought I would be able to live in; this was not one of them. I looked around the four roomed flat (bedroom, bathroom, kitchen and another room which served as a dining/living area). No beds just two mattresses on the floor side-by-side I looked at the cooker it was only partially working. The living room was quite bare.

I tried to ascertain some background information I found out that the gentleman had been estranged from his wife and he had not had much contact with his son who was a virtual stranger. His wife had been killed in front of the young boy and his father had been subjected to torture.

The difficulty was I did my best but as usual it was not good enough. I think I was able to provide some games, so they had something to keep them occupied during the long evenings. But I was dismayed to see there was no TV. I come back to that saying which I quote often. 'Pride goes before a fall'. My memory is hazy, but I seemed to remember negotiating a TV set for them. I went home to Eric pleased as punch telling him about my great victory, they were going to have a TV hopefully a distraction something to watch in the evenings. As pragmatic as ever after a few kind words to me he said yes that is very good but who's going to pay for the TV licence? Back to the drawing board! I had never thought of that.

So so lucky to have Eric to ground me which he does so much of the time! We watched a film together once starring Bing Crosby it was called 'Going my Way'. It was about two priests who were quite different. This is a quote from one of Bing Crosby's movie characters: 'Our methods are different, but our hearts are the same'. Eric said that is us and he is not wrong.

When the Refugee Team was finally disbanded, I retired. But not for long I worked just a morning at a secondary school which was challenging and enjoyable. After that I became an exam invigilator before retiring for good. When my sister said I had had a 'chequered career' she was not wrong!

I rubbed my eyes silly thing to do but they felt itchy and sore. I felt sick (I had just eaten a large packet of vegan crisps) my fault for being so greedy. Plus, my back was aching too, I suppose I had to accept the truth, what I would do with ease at 20 years of age I couldn't necessarily do at 70 plus. And staying up writing until 3 am was one of them.

'I don't think dyslexics are meant to write books' I said it quietly to myself then added 'It is just too hard'. I looked around the floor it was scattered with so many pieces of A4 paper. Some typed on others with handwritten notes, in various coloured ink. Some pages completely full others holding just a sentence or two.

If I had had a mirror, I would have been able to see that I had that expression on my face, the one that I wore when life was puzzling me and I was worried and not sure what to do. Just as I was contemplating whether it was even worth carrying on writing this book. The light went on. Not the actual light but a light in my mind. I had found my title!
I don't think dyslexics are meant to write books!   Hooray time to carry on typing there is a book to be written.

MOOTED TITLES - Some more self-evident than others!

- Have you ever eaten frozen fishfingers?
- Climb your Mountain and never give up
- Electrocution Lessons
- Worry Pot
- Unleashing the memories
- A glimpse into the lifestyle of a dyslexic
- You are a joy and inspiration
- Why is dyslexia not more widely recognised?

PS: The trouble was I then changed my mind AGAIN!! So 'I don't think dyslexics are meant to write books'. It will have to be relegated to 'MOOTED TITLES' as it was supplanted by the one you see on the cover now!

Explanation of new title
Years ago when my nieces were small, my sister went away with her husband on holiday to Africa. I think but I am not sure it was about 2 or 3

weeks. During that time, I went and stayed at their house and looked after my three nieces. Eric was there some of the time, ditto my sister's mother-in-law and the nanny was on hand if I was ever in difficulty.

But most of the time it was me looking after them. The children were amazing they were really good, and I enjoyed looking after them. But (there is always a but isn't there?) I do not like cooking, and I am not very good at it. Plus, as a dyslexic who finds both written and spoken instructions really hard to follow, I dreaded using their oven, microwave, washing machine or tumble dryer.

But I tried my best and thought I had done reasonably well. So, when Lucy the youngest said to me at the time that I'd given her frozen (unthawed) fish fingers for tea one day, I thought nothing of it and that it was a joke, or she was mistaken! They say hindsight is a wonderful thing! I was thinking about this not that long ago while writing this book and the awful realisation came upon me, she might well have been right! So, by way of an apology, I have made that the title of the book.

Chapter 11 - Questions and Answers with a difference

After going to the theatre and having a really enjoyable time sometimes we go home and scratch our heads. We have questions about the author, the plot, or the message that the play is trying to get across. How nice then to come across a theatre that offers you, the audience, an opportunity to speak to the author or the actors afterwards. In what is termed a Q&A session.

Well, here is mine. The only difference is both the questions and answers are, well, mine! A bit unfair sorry but best I can do under the circumstances. I have racked my brains as to what the questions might be. I have made them about dyslexia and then broadened to other topics. I hope you like the results

What is the definition of dyslexia?

Dyslexia means different things to different people depending on a variety of factors. If you know someone who is dyslexic, has been diagnosed with it (like myself) or is in education you will probably be more familiar and accepting of it, although the latter is not a given. However, there is still a lot of scepticism (try spelling that when you are dyslexic, without the aid of Siri) and misunderstanding surrounding it. Here are two opposing viewpoints but more research is urgently needed. It won't surprise you that I concur with the former.

There is a misconception that dyslexia just affects the ability to read and write. If this were true, it would be much easier to identify. In fact, dyslexia can have an effect on areas such as coordination, organisation and memory.

British Dyslexia Association (2021) Signs of dyslexia. Available at: https://www.bdadyslexia.org.uk/dyslexia/about-dyslexia/signs-of-dyslexia (Accessed: 17 September 2021).

Dyslexia May Not Exist, Say Researchers At Yale and Durham Universities

Dyslexia is a "meaningless term", and millions of children may have been wrongly diagnosed, experts at Yale and Durham Universities are claiming in a new book. The academics are calling for the end of the term "dyslexia," which they claim is "unscientific and lacks meaning" the Telegraph reports.

Dyslexia, they say, has become an umbrella term used too frequently for children who display wildly varied reading problems, which ends up wasting resources from putting the children through diagnostic tests.

"Parents are being woefully misled about the value of a dyslexia diagnosis," said Julian Elliot, a professor of education at Durham University who wrote *The Dyslexia Debate* with Yale University professor Elena L. Grigorenko.

Zarrell, R. (2014) Dyslexia may not exist says researchers at Yale and Durham. Available at: https://www.buzzfeednews.com/article/rachelzarrell/dyslexia-may-not-exist-says-researchers-at-yale-and-durham-u (Accessed: 17 September 2021)

Does dyslexia run in families?

There is evidence to suggest that yes it usually runs in families. I have always thought my dad was dyslexic. When he spoke, he often mispronounced words and I don't think writing came easily to him. But then he had missed a lot of schooling due to being run over by a motor bike when he was young and also, I think he left school at 14. Our son was assessed by two educational psychologists. I was assessed by a qualified specialist dyslexic teacher. Therefore, we are both 'officially' dyslexic. Eric has always maintained he is dyslexic (he displays some of the symptoms) but one of the 'unidentified ones' there were/are certainly many of them sadly.

Do deafness and dyslexia go together?

I can only write about our family experience. Certainly, my dad was very deaf. Not sure why possibly from the war. Our son is deaf, but we think that was due to an accident on a firing rang. Eric went deaf suddenly, in one ear, whist on holiday. My deafness happened in my 40s. Eric, our son and I all have hearing aids. We all cope well. Albeit I went to the nurse to be tested when I suspected I was losing my hearing. She tested me then confirmed yes, my hearing was deteriorating.

I started to cry which surprised both her and me. She was taken aback saying 'But you know you are losing your hearing why are you upset?' Hard to explain. But it is one thing to think or suspect something but it's another thing entirely to have it confirmed! But once confirmed I just got on with it the way Dad, Eric and Stu did.

Do more boys than girls have dyslexia?

This is not a definitive answer as it depends on where you get your research from. Traditionally I think it has always been thought that there are more boys than girls with dyslexia and the majority still hold this view. But as far as I can see from looking at various sites this is now being disputed by some people. More research is needed.

Have things improved over time for dyslexics?

I think almost nothing was known about it when my dad was growing up. My dyslexia was certainly not recognised at school. A friend of mine recognised it in me. By the time our son was displaying signs although the state schools he attended did not seem to be able to address this the private sector did. I think there have been improvements but still a lot more needs to be done.

You intimated your mum and dad were very fair minded. How did that transfer to your life? Plus, what did they say about the things you did?

My sister and I were very lucky. I don't think either mum or dad unlike a lot of people we knew at that time, had a racist, prejudice bone in their bodies. I played and become friendly with anyone I wanted to.   My best friend at school was a person of colour. I am not sure they always completely understood why I wanted to do the things I did. Nevertheless, I always had Eric, my parents, our son, my sister, and friends' support. Here is one example. I remember when I learnt about the situation with HIV/AIDS. The awful unfair stigma, fear and prejudice that was attached to it. I decided I wanted to become a buddy (a sort of befriender). I did the training, met some amazing people and started to buddy. His partner knew his status, but his family did not. I will call him R. He loved and was fascinated by aeroplanes. Eric also loved planes and we lived under the flight path. I look back and can see in my mind's eye the two of them sitting in the garden chatting and watching the planes go over. The only thing that mattered to either of them was their joint passion for planes.

When R was taken into a hospice, and I was away for the weekend unable to visit, our son without a second thought said 'yes' when I asked him to visit in my stead.
Once when mum and R came to lunch, and I was in the kitchen. I heard R ask mum what she thought about me being a buddy. I was interested to hear her reply. After some thought she said: 'Well I am a bit surprised as she does not like hospitals'. Typical mum no prejudice just being practical. Oh, and she was right I was a complete coward about hospitals! I also remember an Indian gentleman from dad's work coming round one Sunday morning. I think the only thing that mattered to dad was whether people were nice or not!

When my sister left for Uni, she asked me to take over running the Brownie Pack which she had been running every Friday night which I did but I have to admit very badly. I do not remember a lot about it only that it was dad who came round, and baby sat. Unusual for those times, Mum must have been working. I remember dad saying he would do anything except change nappies. I think if the need arose, he had to go and ask one of the neighbours! Dad was wonderful with Stu, Stu idolised him. They always got on so very well and had such fun and games together. A special relationship.

What are you doing now? Will you ever write another book?

I am having a rest after this book but not for long there is simply always another mountain to conquer but it certainly won't be another book. Somebody said once that everybody has one book in them, and this is mine.

What sort of music do you like?

How long have you got?

- "Imagine" by John Lennon
- "Blinded By Your Grace" by Stormzy
- "Rise of Evil" by Sabaton
- "Someone You Loved" by Lewis Capaldi
- "The Older I Get" by Alan Jackson
- "Annie's song" by John Denver
- "Perfect" by Ed Sheeran
- "Same Love" by Macklemore and Ryan Lewis featuring Mary Lambert

What sort of books do you like reading?

I absolutely adore 'Eleanor Oliphant is perfectly fine'. So uplifting and inspiring. To me it is all about kindness and how it can change lives. I also love Maya Angelou. I have a very good friend/sister Carolyn. She is amazing at finding really unusual, informative and inspiring books. Often with people of colour as the heroine/hero.

What sort of paintings do you like?

I know very little about painting, but I do love Guernica by Picasso. I once travelled all the way to Madrid so I could go into the museum where it was on display. I just stood staring at it scrutinising it for the longest time!

How has being dyslexic affected your life?

I was going to write about all the things I find so difficult living with dyslexia. But the more I tried, and I did try so very hard the more I felt that it was something I just could not put into words. I spent hours, writing things then deleting them, trying again then again being dissatisfied with the result. I could not do it justice. Perhaps it is just too raw and painful.

Finally, I decided not to give up but to be adaptable something I have written about in my final chapter. I have left it to the expert. Please read the report, which was written about me and my dyslexia and is at the back of the book it explains it all much better than I could.

But I would like to say just one thing: We unfortunately had/have woodlice in our conservatory, despite trying to eradicate them. Every morning I look to see if I can spot them and 'report' back to Eric. The trouble is for the life of me I cannot remember the word 'woodlice'. So, I substituted another word, which I think a lot of dyslexics have to do, for the word: beedle bug - for some unfathomable reason I can remember that word!

Well normally at this time someone would say 'Well I think that's all we have got time for'. Instead, I think I'm going to write, well that's all I've got space for. Finally, I want to thank everybody who has read or purchased this book. I hope it did not disappoint.

Jean

Chapter 12 - A Message for Dyslexics

Having someone believe in us and encourage us, always being there for us, telling us we can do it, is worth its weight in gold. They have bequeathed on us a lifetime gift that can get us far. But eventually we have to believe in ourselves, other people's belief in us, has to transform into self-belief. Even then, the reality for dyslexics is not that simple. Dyslexia is still very misunderstood and sadly not everybody has someone behind them who is supportive. So, the step to self-belief can be even more difficult. Unlike me please do not spend a lifetime thinking you are stupid or slow you're not you're dyslexic. We sometimes have to be brave enough to explain.

Your way of doing it is the traditional way I respect that but it's not my way. My way is different I am doing it the only way I know how, the way that works for me. Please could you try to understand and respect that? Yes, we sometimes have to adapt. The status quo might not allow us to change things or to do it our way. So, then we have to find a way around it. We have to be adaptable.

There are many things that are essential for dyslexics when growing up. Early diagnosis and the right help are crucial. However just as important are role models, to inspire us. If they can do it so can we! Throughout history, up to modern day there are and have been many famous dyslexics that have been high achievers. They have left and are still leaving their mark. I researched online and found the following who are 'cited' as dyslexic. But it would be advisable to do your own research. The internet has been known to be wrong!

Walt Disney - Creator of Micky Mouse, Donald Duck, Disneyland/World

Antonia Morosi - Chef Entrepreneur

Albert Einstein - Scientist who discovered the theory of relativity

Keira Knightly - Actress

John Lennon – Singer, Musician, Songwriter, Peace Activist

Holly Willoughby – Presenter, Author

Jamie Oliver - Chef Restaurateur

Whoopi Goldberg – Comedian, Actress, Author

Leonardo da Vinci – Inventor, Painter, Designer

Lastly, I have a really important message for you never, ever, ever give up on your dream, good luck! I want to end with a poem. It is one of my most favourite poems in the whole world.

Sometimes

Sometimes things don't go, after all, from bad to worse.
Some years, muscadel faces down frost; green thrives; the crops don't fail.
Sometimes a Man aims High, and all goes well.
A people sometimes will step back from war; elect an honest man; decide they care enough, that they can't leave some stranger poor.
Some men become what they were born for.
Sometimes our best efforts do not go amiss; sometimes we do as we meant to. The sun will sometimes melt a field of sorrow that seemed hard frozen: may it happen for you

I contacted the poet, and I was granted permission to use the poem providing I did not name the poet.

Specific Learning Difficulties (Dyslexia/Dyscalculia) Assessment Report

Dyslexia is a learning difficulty that primarily affects the skills involved in accurate and fluent word reading and spelling. Characteristic features of dyslexia are difficulties with phonological awareness, verbal memory, and verbal processing speed. It is best thought of not as a distinct category and there are no clear cut off points. Co-occurring difficulties may be seen in aspects of language, motor co-ordination, mental calculation, concentration, and personal organisation, but these are not themselves markers of dyslexia.

Identifying and teaching Children and Young People with Dyslexia and Literacy Difficulty (page 10 and 30) by Jim Rose

Assessment of Jean Swain

Date of Birth: *6.4.50*

Date of Assessment: *18th January 2013*

Qualifications: *BEd, PG Diploma in Special and Inclusive Education*

Overview, conclusions, and recommendations

Background

I am a qualified Dyslexia Teacher with British Dyslexia Approved Teacher Status. I have worked with Jean as a teaching colleague for over twenty years. Since gaining a Diploma in SPLD I have identified Jean as displaying many of the characteristics of Dyslexia and Dyscalculia. Jean has now asked for a formal assessment; due to the challenges she is facing studying for her Maths GCSE.

Dyslexia is known to run in families. Jean's father was probably dyslexic, Jean can see her literacy, maths and memory challenges, mirroring that of her father. Her husband is dyslexic and their son, is severely dyslexic, which resulted in him attending a specialist dyslexic secondary school in Cranbrook Kent.

Since childhood, Jean has a horror of not doing the right thing. At school Jean was kept in at playtimes for not doing enough work but this was not the case. The irony is that Jean was probably putting in far more effort than her peers due to her underlying difficulties. She describes how she was, "painstakingly making sure that I was reading and then following the instructions correctly". Even now, Jean constantly reads and re-read instructions in case she makes a mistake.

Jean's academic achievements: a Teaching Degree and Post Graduate Diploma in Immigration Law, show her academic abilities to be above average. Jean worked for many years in the education system as a Refugee and Asylum Seeker Adviser, having started her career as a class teacher. The role allowed Jean a level of autonomy and ways of working which were more flexible than school-based teaching, which suited Jean's learning style. Retrospectively however Jean reflects on the hours and hours she has spent writing reports for pupils which took so much longer than those written by her colleagues.

Phonological processing

Phonological processing difficulties are an indicator of dyslexia. Jean displays difficulties with phonological processing skills which are reflected in her speech, reading and spelling. Jean often mispronounces words. She says words which are out of context in sentences because they sound similar to the word she is looking for, pronounces words incorrectly or mixes up the phonology of words. In this assessment for example Jean said "cish and fips" instead of 'fish and chips.

Jean has developed many successful strategies in her adult life to help her cope with the reading demands placed on her in her work and daily life. Again, this involves Jean planning in advance if she needs to say longer words which are challenging. An example of this was when Jean knew she would need to say the word millennium with a group of children. To learn it she split it down into syllables and repeated it over and over again, with increasing speed, until she learnt it. This is a common way I have taught students with dyslexia to learn spellings. If words are too difficult Jean will substitute a simpler word if possible. When reading a passage Jean left out the words she couldn't pronounce, even though this meant that the meaning was lost. When questioned afterwards her recall of the text was not strong. This is due to the fact that so much effort has been used decoding words that Jean had lost the meaning of the text. When reading Jean says she often has to re-read sections to clarify the meaning.

Jean finds the computer has helped her spelling and composition, although there are occasions when she reads back her writing and it does not make sense, she has to re-write it. I looked at Jean's notebooks and she omits words when writing and typing and sometimes repeats words. Her writing is hard to read.
Although not a dyslexia indicator Jean confuses left and right, b and p and c and g. She has lived at the same address 'Waddington Way' for 30 years, but still writes it as 'Wadding Way'.

We read though some GCSE maths paper and Jean was confused about the meanings of words and how to start questions. Her approach was neither logical nor systematic. I could see why she was concerned about her slow progress with her maths GCSE coursework.

Verbal processing speed

Verbal processing speed is another characteristic of SPLD. When speaking it was noticed that Jean became flustered and tripped over her words, she describes speech as "not coming naturally to me". For these reasons Jean spends a lot of time rehearsing what she is going to say. When typing Jean enjoys the fact that she can use words that she would not use when speaking.

Working memory and short-term memory

Another common feature of SPLD is short term memory and working memory. Short term memory affects our ability to remember things and working memory our ability to hold facts and then use them. They are commonly tested by digit span recall forward and backwards. Jean's score was below average on both of these tests. This will affect her ability to remember facts and numbers, to remember what to do with the facts and numbers she is presented with and to organise information. Practically when Jean transposes long numbers like phone numbers for example, she has devised a method to check she is writing them correctly. Her system is to check them forward and then backwards. For example, "67890123 I check forward 67.... then backward 32 Jean has noticed that she takes much, much longer to do things than other people.

At traffic lights Jean has made her own memory prompts, to help her remember the sequence of what to do. For example, she remembers 'green' means 'go' because both green and go begin with a 'g'. When approaching traffic lights, she constantly repeats "g for go, g for green". Jean remembers the accelerator pedal is on the right by saying "right to go". At times during the assessment Jean became very muddled and reported that sometimes after concentrating hard she has a headache. Jean described herself as, "having a slow ploddy pace because I am constantly checking things to make sure I am doing the correct thing even emailing. I try so hard to be organised but find it very difficult to be organised".

Recommendations

From my assessment of Jean, I have established that Jean has SPLD in the areas of dyslexia and dyscalculia. She copes remarkably well with her daily life, but her self-esteem and confidence are affected on a daily basis. Jean spends many nights up late writing reports and carrying out homework which she checks and re-checks. To read, write, speak and remember and use facts requires far more effort than for her non-dyslexic, non-dyscalculic peers.

Although Jean's literacy difficulties were more easily identified though my assessments her difficulties with maths were also evident. Jean did not draw cues form written maths questions which I would have expected. Her working memory made it extremely challenging for her to follow mathematical operations through logically and sequentially.

Whereas as Jean has taught herself strategies to remember day to day tasks such as what to do at traffic lights and checking her reading and writing constantly, these strategies have not been developed for maths. Jean's learning style shows that she responds well to planning pre-teaching and over learning. Jean is an intelligent woman who is struggling to achieve her potential in maths. Jean is spurred on by challenges rather than being defeated by them and has great perseverance. As a result, I would recommend that Jean receives targeted SPLD support with her maths GCSE, so that she is better able to access the curriculum. This could take the form of one to one or group support. I would also recommend additional time during exams for reading and processing question

Author's Apologies

Hands up I found out something about myself that I don't really like, I'm vain. Also, impatient and in my defence just plain tired. I had had this book proof-read but then I altered some things and I added and omitted others. In reality I should have left it alone or arranged for it to be proof-read again. But I was anxious having taken so so long writing it, to get it published.

I must have re-read it 50 times looking for errors. I thought that was enough and that there could not possibly be any mistakes left. I forgot about the nature of dyslexia I apologise.

Once I had it published and got a physical copy in my hand and re-read it both Eric and I could see errors. Interestingly and fortunately not the same ones. These have now been corrected.

However sadly that does not mean that all the errors have been corrected. I am tempted to do what I used to do with the worksheets that I made when I taught. No matter how hard I tried and how many times I altered things inevitably the students would find at least one mistake. In the end I used to add something like: "Can you find the deliberate mistake?"

It seems I should have added that to this book. A little birdie told me that my nieces think that it was half frozen chicken nuggets not fish fingers that I tried to make them eat.

There is every likelihood they are right, given my dyslexic memory. If so, I apologise. There is a slight chance that we are both right as cooking in a strange oven for me was a nightmare and chances are they got more than one half cooked or uncooked meal. Or and this is highly unlikely they are wrong and I am right.

Anyway please keep informing me of any questions/mistakes etc and I will try to address them.

In the early days of women's liberation, I used to visit a building and as I went up the stairs I would look to my right and see the quote below. Which I found inspiring! I'm not quite sure how I came to have it in my possession but it hangs on my wall to this day and inspires me to take risks which is what I did when I wrote this book.

Even after the effort it took as a dyslexic to write this book, I would still urge any other dyslexic to write if that is what they need/want to do.

Good luck!
Jean

"When a woman friend or colleague tries to be assertive and makes a mess of it, that is the moment she needs your support and congratulations for having taken the risk."

Anne Dickson

Printed in Great Britain
by Amazon